twinge

noun

/ˈtwinj/

1. A sudden, sharp, localized pain.

The twinge of grief is felt in the same places love hits first.

poems, prose and stories

SIGNED, A.B.

Published by Glass Spider Publishing
www.glassspiderpublishing.com
Cover design by Judith S. Design & Creativity
www.judithsdesign.com
Copy Editor and Typesetter Vince Font

GLASS**SPIDER**PUBLISHING

*For every person who showed me love,
especially in the years that I was small and
moldable—know that I keep it with me, always.*

In memory of Helen Anne Tripp

*Signed,
A.B..*

twinge

noun

/ˈtwinj/

1. A sudden, sharp, localized pain.

The twinge of grief is felt in the same places love hits first.

Everything that has ever hurt,
be it the wasp
after it was stepped on,
the foot that meddled around the wild
flower,
the first petal that falls
after the stem was chopped at the ankle
and displayed in a clear vase
for everyone to see
the damage –

Everything that has ever hurt
has known comfort,
felt the sun kiss its cheek.
Be it the ruthless pollinator,
the child finding wishes in the grass,
the rose just stretching its arms
after a winter nap,
or you

observer of lightning storms,
blood-pumping, beating magnet,
finger that has been pricked,
cheekbone that has been damp

You,
midnight happy hour,
cold-on-one-side bedsheet,
receiver of fist-blown kiss,
you, too, know about
the snuggle of the quiet
when it isn't yelling.

When I was a kid, I would flip to a page in the dictionary.

I'd haul the book the size of the world to my grandma

and ask her to read me the words and the definitions.

She'd take a magnifying glass to the paper and

use the pinhole of vision she had left after the stroke

to pluck the magic from it, letter by letter,

and pass it to me through sound waves and pencil shavings.

I'd take the words from Grammy's hands like a family heirloom,

use them on scrap envelopes and in jokes and in the wrong places.

I'd duplicate them and give them to everyone around me

like the cheap version of a designer bag.

I knew the magic still stuck to pleather
as long you got it from Grammy's dictionary –
the big red one with a duct taped spine

with the answers to the newspaper crossword
puzzle
nestled inside.

After years of collecting definitions,
what does one do with all of the extra words?

My First Book: A Eulogy

It was pieces of printer paper I had stapled together into a booklet, (which would be a skill that came in handy later as a broke artist,) creatively titled, "The Cheese." It took me hours to make, etching the words into the pages with a pencil like I was trying to carve them out and sketching illustrations that I would later coat in crayon wax. I wrote stories by the dozens each week. I can imagine the countertops and filing cabinets littered with plots and character descriptions and made-up song lyrics, had my family members not been filing them away to be eventually lost in storage or the trash can. The Cheese, however, survived decades. My grandma kept everything. I'm sure she was responsible for the original preservation of the book, but it somehow ended up back with me along the way for eternal hoarding. It's followed me through moves and job changes. It avoided the paper shredder and the broom. It feels like an antique that I gifted to myself, a monument of a time and a person in a different body. My first book was an ode I didn't know I was writing. It was a prerequisite to a lifetime of wondering, a necessary exercise on inquisitiveness.

A brief synopsis: Two mice are having a conversation. Mouse #1 can't stop dreaming about the ball of cheese in the sky and coming up with ideas for how to get up there and get it. He is hungry and passionate. Mouse #2 is looking to the sky, seeing no cheese, and listening to the desperation of Mouse #1. Mouse #1 insists that his dreams are reachable and Mouse #2 won't agree. It occurs to Mouse #2 that the ball of cheese Mouse #1 wants so badly, is simply the moon. Mouse #2 tells little Mouse #1 the tough news that there was no cheese to reach for and even if there was, he could never get to it. The book ended there.

But, what if it hadn't? What if the story of two mice that I wrote when I was 7 continued on?

What if it was a metaphor about myself? How I'll never be convinced that I couldn't build stairs to the moon? Or maybe it is bigger than me. Maybe The Cheese could tell us something about people and our world. What if the moral always was: we can't solve hunger by arguing about what's in the sky?

Or maybe it is just a silly story written by a small girl. Maybe the two mice really just stopped talking about it and it never came up again.

Dear Daydreamer

I know about the sunbeams too.
I've been there, in that field, where the soil
wears its hair in wildflower curls.
I've smelt the crisp pine in the air and heard
the river rushing between rocks.
I've been barefoot in that grass.

I've watched that same action film.
I've played all the characters;
The hero that scales the building,
the villain running from the explosion and
their own consequences,
and the supporting role gasping at the scene.

I've rewritten the lyrics to the song also.
I sang it in a stadium and on the sidewalks of
a city
where everyone is walking fast.

I've found pictures in the ceiling we are
sitting under too.

substitute

School felt like a vicious monster when I was young, which surprised nearly everyone who knew me. I was a curious child, eager to learn and filled to the brim with "fun facts" I'd put in my pockets for a rainy day. I would cry on my way to elementary school every morning and beg my mom to let me stay home. I would hide in the closet or behind the furniture, because I thought that maybe she'd think I had already gone. (Despite being 6 years old and unable to drive.) The truth was: It had nothing to do with school itself and instead, had everything to do with the fact that I was terrified of interacting with unfamiliar people. School was loud and socially demanding. My two best friends at home were my neighbors, and at school, they were in different classes than me. My grandma wasn't there. My mom wasn't there. My brothers weren't there. I felt out of place and confused about the dynamics of it all. I struggled to make friends and speak up. My family deemed me "shy" and "reserved" but it always felt bigger than that. I felt unsafe and couldn't figure out why.

One day, as I sat in the school cafeteria, tuning out the noise and drinking a juice box, a voice broke through the wall I had built up around me. I turned around to see my mom standing there, with a lunch tray of food. She smiled and sat down and asked me about my day. I ate lunch with someone else for the first time that day. When lunch was over, the worry set back in. I would now have to face the playground. I showed my mom where to leave her child-sized tray and made my way to the door that led outside. I expected her to walk the other way, but instead, she said "What do you want to do for recess?" We quietly played in the sand together and in those moments, I did not feel like I had to prove myself to anyone. I could just exist quietly as I always had before. My mom came to lunch and recess with me for about a week, each day giving me words of encouragement about being myself and ideas about how to relieve some of the pressure of fitting in. Eventually, I made friends with the other kids who stayed alone at school. We didn't talk and mostly just did activities next to one another. I survived 4 years, slowly adding on friends as I went. That is, until we had to move.

The news that we were losing our house came unexpectedly, or so it felt to me. I was a kid with no understanding of financial struggle or banks. We moved in with a family member and I switched to a school a few cities away. The fear came back, but this was different than it had been at my old school. I wasn't just the "weird quiet kid" anymore that all of my school mates had come to know. I was the "weird, quiet, new kid" and a group of kids at this school did not take that well. I was met with my first, true bullies – like the kind you learn about in those pamphlets. The monster grew back its teeth, only sharper this time. No matter how many calls my mom made to the school, it didn't change, so I decided I would have to instead. I started trying to act differently, talk differently, wear different clothes. I tried anything to avoid their eyes.

On a random Wednesday, our teacher let us know that she would be out the next day, so we would be doing the activity I hated the very most with a substitute; Reading out loud. One by one, each kid in the class would have to read a paragraph from a book we were reading as a group with a small microphone attached to them. Everyone would be paying attention, listening, watching and the teacher who had come to know us all would not be there to lead. Not only that, but the bullies were meaner when our teacher wasn't around. I left school dreading the next day, thinking about how I would make it through. I was older now, but felt the smallest I ever had. I went to sleep in a panic.

I woke up, got dressed and hopped in the car with my mom. She drove my brother and I to school and dropped us off as normal with a smile and a wave as we shut the car door. I walked in, went to my classroom and sat in my seat. We all waited, watching the door for our teacher-for-the-day. I heard the footsteps and looked up, only to see my mom with a notebook in her hand. She said, "Hi, everyone. I will be your substitute today. Please take your seats so we can begin class." My own mom went and sat at the desk and grabbed out the microphone for the public reading assignment. She didn't tell anyone she was my parent. She called on me just like everyone else in the class. It was almost a silent act of solidarity, a motivational speech that only her and I knew about. It was an act of love so strong, I felt my brain cells adjust positions. I read my paragraph, with a shaky voice and all. We did a math worksheet. She told us it was time to go outside, so I did what I knew how to do – I went outside and found the other kid who was alone. I mustered up every ounce of courage I could find and asked if she wanted to sit in the grass together. We went far away from everyone else and sat down next to one another. We picked at the blades quietly for 45 minutes.

I sit at my desk job,
pull the pink pen
from an array of corporate blue and black
and write a poem on a sticky note.
My boss catches me thinking in pixie dust
instead of professionalism
and tells me to get back to work.
I flinch and put the scribbled-on square
into a filing cabinet,
with every other beautiful thing
turned melancholy
that I have created here.
I glance at the standard notebook
the supply room gave me
for reminder notes and phone numbers.
I call it a tease.
I tell it I am homesick.
I ask it if it gets bored
of the life it was told
it needed to have.
I ask myself too.
I get back to work.

The First Winter After Depression Let Me Go

I had always preferred warmth to
the static and bite of the snow,
but this storm was lighter and softer than any
before it.
The dark was okay – kind even.
I could hear the tree branches calling out,
encouraging me to rest
as they do.
I could feel the breeze brushing my cheek,
like a hand wiping the leak
from my faucet eyes.

Winter was not cruel and cold, as I had
believed for so long.
It was calm and nurturing.
It was hushed and thoughtful.
The Winter was a meditation guide,
speaking only in the moments I needed to be
reminded
to breathe.

I thanked the sky
for sending me this fluttering gift of solace.

I stood still as stone, watching as the drift
replaced red and orange with bright white.

I wondered how I had never watched the
snowflakes slow dance.
I questioned how I hadn't seen placid waters
turn into a floor before.
I marveled at the idea of Winter being
anything but warm.

The ink of Winter I had dreaded for so long,
didn't belong to Winter at all.
It was my own heartache, placing its body in
front of the window at each snowfall.

So, I thanked the sky again.

my dad's squirrels

He stops to take a photo each time one
scurries past. He had a feeder once, shaped
like a little bench for the friend in the yard to
sit on and eat seeds. He is a burly, bearded,
blue collar, swing-a-hammer type of dad, so
the contrast surprises people sometimes. He
turns to a child who's just seen snow for the
first time when the bushy-tailed critters
appear and he'll watch them as they glitch
around, scattering food and scaling trees. He
works a tough job, my dad. It is physically
laborious and takes him out of town every
other week. He lives in a trailer when he's
gone which is decorated like a fort with a
"NO GIRLS ALLOWED" sign on the door.
There are empty snack containers full of bolts
and screws where the picture frames should
go and a duffel bag full of clothes right next
to the dresser. He has to tell other men what
to do and where to do it and he gets the job
done. But, once in a while, he'll send a photo,
right in the middle of his long shifts outside
in the weather; A squirrel, peeking from

behind a rock. I imagine him putting down his tools and wiping grease from his eyes to admire it. I wonder if his work guys see my dad, or if they see the teenager in him, still trying to toughen up and suck it up and man up the way men are told to. I've always seen both. He's strong and stern and loving and thoughtful.

He met my mom when I was just a toddler, waddling around the room and giggling at noise. She was an edgy and beautiful single mom to a little girl and he was a cool guy with cool friends, also divorced, with two boys. They met young. They both had pasts and struggles and pain to unpack. In the coming years, my biological father would ask to have his name taken off of my birth certificate, but none of us knew that yet. It didn't matter. We were just a group of people with mismatched DNA, who acted like this was the plan all along.

I was still young the first time he went out of town for work. I was newly a step-daughter and big sister to my parents' first and only biologically shared child. My mom walked with two small kids to the mailbox, pulled out the stack of bills and junk. She rummaged through it and happily pulled out one piece to hand to me, saying "Look! You got mail!" Getting mail as a kid felt like winning the lottery. Nothing could make me feel as big. I grabbed one of the only postcards I would ever receive from anyone and read the back, embellished with my name and our home address.

> *Hey sweetie!*
> *Made it to New York. I miss you!*
> *I'll be back soon.*
> *Love,*
> *Dad*

Straight from the Big Apple; Home to the Statue of Liberty and the Empire State Building – He had sent me a postcard with a picture of a squirrel on it
and signed it, "dad"

To be the sister of brothers

is to be porcelain in the highest cabinet,
a book with the dust sleeve still on,
the hands of the clock in its glass castle
surrounded by roman numeral guard posts.

It is to be in a box made of metal when the
lightning strikes,
on the bridge above the river when the sun
comes out to melt the ice,
under the umbrella when the sky falls down.

To be the sister of brothers
is to become the water in the pot,
a boiling rage
and still stay under the lid.

To be the sister of brothers
is to be a wooden table
always draped in cloth

and to be the brothers of a sister
is to be deemed strong
even in moments you are made of soft clay

because she knows
I know
all it takes is fire.

My Grandma, The Prince

I wanted to be a princess. I'd put on my grandma's gowns to drown in and high heeled shoes that my tiny feet only filled the toes of. The old radio played Classical music from one of the fuzzy stations. My grandma would draw on a curly mustache above her upper lip and invite me to the ball in the living room. My eyes would correct the scenery – The carpet turned to marble, the ceiling raised to a muraled vault, the fan grew tangled crystal arms. We'd choreograph on the spot, as proper as the poor knew how. After each dance, she'd take a bow and I'd do a curtsy.

When I was 18, I had my first girlfriend. Telling my grandma scared me. I knew she loved me, but others her age had told me I'd burn.

When I blurted it out, after a long lead up on how I hoped she wouldn't be disappointed and I was scared to lose her, she laughed,

"I guess I didn't need to draw on the mustache."

and the two mice never talked about it again.

My hands don't look like my hands.
They look older, with more spots and creases.
My nails are manicured.
My fingers are decorated with rings and a
bandage from a papercut.
There was a time that the injury would have
bothered me more.
I would have held my broken skin with the
other untouched hand.
I would have ran to my mother, sobbing and
begging for the magic of knowing
it would eventually stop stinging.
There was a time when this tiny accident
would be shattering –
or maybe there was a time that it was okay to
be hurt and be loud about it.
Maybe there was a time when my hands were
small and full of wonder and fragile.

Now, i'm here, calloused and sore from
decades of making things
with a cut at the tip of my aged finger,

that I bubbled with peroxide and silently covered up.

I spent so long believing my hands would never grow old.
I think about my friends that live there, in our youth.
We clung to one another like clothes static from the dryer,
high and angsty and brave.
I remember them.
16 year old hands,
eternally scarred with a lighter burn and cracked knuckles.
22 year old hands,
parched from days in the sunshine and holding onto hope.
26 year old hands,
had only just stopped growing.

It makes me wish they could see their hands old too.

There Was a Last Time

My little brother pulled up on his bike and
told me to jump on the pegs.
My middle brother and I stopped to get a
doughnut with pocket change.
My oldest brother's baseball hit my bright
pink glove.
A couple of us cousins turned the yard into a
bakery
and made pies out of twigs and mud in
Grammy's good pans.
My best friends and I sat on a blanket at the
skatepark.
The world was both the smallest and the
biggest it would ever be
at the same time.

We had no idea it would be the last time,
and then we were grown up.

I've looked for love in all the wrong places
and to my surprise
I've found it.
In the unlit corners
and the end of the alley.
I've found it hiding in the back rooms
and in the basements.
I've found love in the most loveless places –
The space between the gasp
and the attempt to retrieve a forgotten name,
in the dingy bathroom
with the music still pounding on the door.
Love doesn't listen to boundaries.
It will nestle itself between you and a
stranger.
It will throw its arm in an almost-closed
elevator.
It will sit right next to you on an otherwise
empty bus.
It clings to the bottom of my shoe.
It is the receipt in my coat pocket.
It is the penny in the parking lot.
It is pet hair on my clothes.
Love is always there
somewhere

Short Ode to the Family Garden

You, built from an old shovel
and a little bit of everyone.
You, fresh parsley, snap peas,
and raspberry bush emptied at the first sight
of fruit.
You, old seeds found in the bed of the truck,
new seeds blown over from the neighbor's
yard,
surprise sprouts from years prior.
You, venue for an unplanned family
gathering,
all-types-of-birds landing pad,
and dancefloor for the butterflies –

You are responsible for so much blooming.

My pockets have always been full.
Pebbles and acorns,
paperclips bent into new shapes,
an earring I'll never find the match to
just in case.

I display my collections,
arrange them just so.
A small dish of bobby pins
goes next to a torn handkerchief folded in a
square
goes next to an old doll from home
goes next to a drawing of a house and a tree
and so on

I am a victim of sentiment –
old packing boxes full of letters,
a phone full of voicemails,
a handful of names
of people I met once
and a drawer full of names
of people I met twice
and a life full of people I'll miss forever.

The Last Story I Ever Wrote for My Grandma
*an excerpt from her obituary (2021)

Helen enjoyed working in her yard and planting her garden. She loved black coffee and crossword puzzles and could beat anyone in a game of Scrabble or a dance battle. Her skills in the kitchen were unmatched and everyone looked forward to eating at her house. She taught her grandchildren to hula-hoop and do cartwheels. Helen created a sanctuary in her home, which everyone was welcome to find peace and comfort in.

Helen was quick-witted and well-spoken. She was intelligent and filled to the brim with words found in her favorite dictionary, which she held onto, despite the pages being bent and torn.

Dear Poet,

Despite your everdancing
wrist and steady breath,
right between the line
you like and the (almost) rhym-
ing one, smashed in a small space
or a large

gap,
you will find bad days.

You will be **c** funeral **ut** organ
or an **o** ambulance **ff** siren.

You will be swallowed
  by the gut of a heavy
  blanket, the kind that
   begs you not to set
        an alarm.

You will be interrupted

by the scent of an ex-lover's
bed sheet or your late
grandmother's perfume

and in that quiet place,
the pen will bargain with you.
Take it's offer,
even if it isn't reasonable.
Or don't.
But, remember that in the case
you decline it's efforts to
persuade you back,
it will always be there
calling for your hands
and how thoughtful a gesture:
to turn itself microphone
for you

I'm afraid grief is a dandelion.
Nothing has ever been
as fluffed full of wishes
as loss is.
Nothing sprinkles itself
across a whole field
the way that a goodbye
you did not want to say
does.

Grief digs its arms deep
into the soil
and lets its fingers widen
the size of the garden hose,
becomes the big hand
holding the small hand
of its loved one beside it
and grasps
like they are waiting
on good news.

The yellow of it is brief,
but it lights up the walk.
A glimpse of before
blooms for only a moment
and smiles back at you

while you remember
before it turns itself seed
and flutters elsewhere.

There are sprays and powders,
tools and tricks,
companies and advertisements
designed to get rid of it,
but the truth is,
those who named it a weed
had never dug to the root
and made a tea of it.

Had they,
they'd know that grief has always been
love that is trying to keep growing
where it always had before,
but the damn lawn
keeps getting in the way.

About the Author

Angelika Brewer is a writer and creativity enthusiast from Ogden, Utah, where she was named the City Poet Laureate from 2022-2026. Angelika comes from a family of Czechoslovakian immigrants who, upon arriving to the United States, began the generational tradition of working for the railroad. Her love of Ogden and its history, both on its own and as a familial symbol, inspires much of her work as an artist and community organizer.

Angelika is responsible for the public installation *The Ogden Ar(t)chives Mailbox*, where visitors can submit creations to be historically archived through the City of Ogden. She teaches creative writing skills courses through multi-medium arts with the Ogden Contemporary Arts: The Artist Factory program, and she visits schools and groups across Utah to share ideas on creativity. Angelika was named an Academy of American Poets Poet Laureate Fellow in 2024.